"To be scientific does not mean to be infallible, but it means being clear and honest, and as exact as we know how to be."

- Sir Oliver Lodge, F.R.S.

# ONE LAST THING!

Strange, curious and humorous
conversations with the other side.

Collected and compiled by

## John E.L. Tenney

Cover photograph by ScooterZen
Sydney, Austrailia

Interior photographs by John E.L. Tenney unless otherwise noted.

One Last Thing!
*Strange, curious and humorous conversations with the other side.*

First Edition
ISBN 978-1468101775

# Preface

I will assume that anyone reading this book already has at least a general understanding of the quasi-experimental process know as E.V.P. or electronic voice phenomena. Countless numbers of "samples" can be found around the internet and heard on paranormal "reality" shows. Usually these pieces of so-called evidence sound horrible and, in almost every sense, are terrible. Many of the recordings are overly manipulated by audio programs or are just plain faked. For the amount of "investigators" who perform E.V.P. sessions a very large majority usually have no knowledge of how and or why the process is supposed to work. I've encountered hundreds of people who have been performing E.V.P. sessions who have no idea that the concept is well over 60 years old. Indeed, using some sort of "technology" to attempt contact with the alleged spirit world has been going on for centuries.

The process I am most comfortable using is one that was pioneered by the likes of Raudive and Jürgenson. I use analog recorders and cassette or reel-to-reel tapes. Much like Raudive many of my recordings contain multiple languages and are surprisingly very clear with most needing nothing more than slight volume or speed adjustments. Also my recordings contain more than just one word responses to questions. I am in possession of many tapes that contain full sentences which answer thoroughly, yet sometimes cryptically, my questions.[1]

Over the past two decades I have been either been involved with, hosted or investigated hundreds, if not thousands of E.V.P. sessions and still to this day I often feel silly while they are going on.[2] Asking questions aloud to what seems to be an empty room for hours on end can very quickly test your patience and dedication to the investigative process. Sometimes, most times actually, there is nothing usable or interesting upon reviewing the recording. Yet, when a response is clear it makes all of the self-consciousness, all of the doubt, all of the skepticism worthwhile.

As I was attempting to catalog my files, which includes hundreds of taped E.V.P. sessions, I began looking over the transcripts I had made from the attempts which had yielded some sort of results. I found in many instances there were very humerous responses from "the other side" and for as funny as they seemed to be there were just as many that were not only intensely creepy but were so curiously vague and I felt they needed to be shared with a larger audience.

Make no mistake, this book is meant to entertain and hopefully spark a much

---

1. Please remember while reading the follow pages that due to the method of E.V.P. I am performing I do not hear the responses until after the session is over and I am reviewing the recording.
2. See page 54

needed debate about, not only the process of technological communication with what is believed by many to be the phantasmagorical but, the larger and more important questions regarding the nature of human existence and the process of dying. I would also like to ask other researchers to try and incorporate some of the responses I have printed here. Over the years I have found that certain specific terms actually increase the chances of receiving a response. As an example, across many years and various locations I have discovered that quite a number of "entities" use the terms "Always" and "Forever" as the distinct name of the place they believe themselves to be located. When I do E.V.P. sessions now, I find that by using the terms I have heard from "the other side" a strange rapport can be built which, sometimes, seems to increase the amount and clarity of the responses that are found by the examiner afterwards.

As an interesting side note to the traditional methods of performing E.V.P. I have also found that "thinking" a question will sometimes garner responses. Although this takes a large amount of concentration, to clear the mind of distractions and focus solely on the question at hand, it raises a myriad of questions. Such as:

Do "ghosts" really "hear" us?

How do "ghosts" hear us?

Are "ghosts" psychic?

Is the realm where "ghosts" exist purely thought-based?

...and far more questions than I can list here.

I of course am using the word "ghost(s)" in a general manner. The questions apply to any and all supposed entities which may inhabit some portion of our existence.

Far too many times researchers, investigators, ghost-hunters and the generally interested get caught up in the "freak out" factor which so dominates our everyday world when we discuss the "paranormal." Hopefully one day we can use all the information and data, which has been examined and collected in an appropriate manner, to start moving the conversation and debate into a more serious tone. We are after all dealing with the greatest questions humanity has ever known.

For now though, read the following pages and enjoy the fun, freaky and sometimes frightening responses that have been spoken to us by those without mouths in a world, which to us, is as yet undiscovered.

John E.L. Tenney

Fall 2011

# The Smart Aleck

Researcher: How did you die?

Voice: *What makes you think I'm dead?*

Researcher: Are you here with me?

Voice: *No.*

Researcher: Can I do to anything help you?

Voice: *You can't even see me.*

Recording made March 12, 2005
Detroit, Michigan

# The Brat

..............................................................................

Researcher: Can you make a sound for me?

Voice: **Boo**

Researcher: This device helps me hear you?

Voice: **It's junk.**

Researcher: What is your name?

Voice: **A ghost.**

Researcher: How old are you?

Voice: **Now or then?**

..............................................................................

Recording made June 1, 2007
Cleveland, Ohio

# Just Waking Up

Researcher: Is there anyone here with me?

Voice: *Go away*

Researcher: I'd like to talk to you.

Voice: *It's early.*

Researcher: You can talk into this machine.

Voice: *Where's my pillow?*

Researcher: Can you hear me?

Voice: *All too well.*

Recording made January 16, 2003
Monroe, Michigan

# Just Plain Mean

·····················································································

Researcher: I'd like to speak with you.

Voice: *This again?*

Researcher: I know it's hard to communicate.

Voice: *For you.*

Researcher: Can you see me?

Voice: *That coat is ugly.*

*Responses translated from French.*

·····················································································

Recording made August 10, 2005
Chicago, Illinois

# What?

Researcher: There are some people here who would like to talk to you.

Voice: *What?*

Researcher: We're going to ask you some questions.

Voice: *What?*

Researcher: Take as much time as you need to respond.

Voice: *I must be going deaf.*

Recording made May 12, 2008
Alpena, Michigan

# The Hungry Ghost?

Researcher: We don't mean any harm or disrespect.

Voice: *The girl has gum*

Researcher: We are willing to stay here with you all night.

Voice: *Does anyone have snacks?*

Researcher: We would like it if you would talk to us.

Voice: *(moaning sound)*

Researcher: Is there anything we can do for you?

Voice: *Get dinner*

*One girl in the group was chewing gum at the time of the E.V.P. session.*

Recording made November 15, 2003
Toledo, Ohio

# Very Funny

........................................................................................

Researcher: If you can hear me can you
knock like this...
*(Knocks on the floor twice)*

Voice: **Who's there?**

Researcher: Repeat Please.

Voice: **Repeat Please Who?**

........................................................................................

Recording made December 2, 2001
Dallas, Texas

# Family Ties

Researcher: Your brother would like to talk to you.

Voice: *Where's my sister?*

Researcher: Do you want to speak to him?

Voice: *No... My sister.*

Researcher: Your brother wants you to know he misses you.

Voice: *I miss my sister.*

Researcher: Your whole family misses you.

Voice: *Bring my sister next time.*

*The client's sister was in Europe at the time of the EVP session.*

Recording made June 9, 2009
Kalamazoo, Michigan

# Creepy

........................................................................................

Researcher: Where do you think you are?

Voice: *In the forever.*

Researcher: Is anyone there with you?

Voice: *All everyone no one.*

Researcher: What do you see where you are?

Voice: *The always.*

........................................................................................

Recording made July 23, 2006
Detroit, Michigan

# Talk about Death

...................................................................................................

Researcher: Can you answer some
        questions for me?

Voice: *I'll wait.*

Researcher: I would really appreciate your
        help in making contact.

Voice: *You're on your way.*

Researcher: Can I do anything to make
        contact between us easier?

Voice: *Time takes care of that.*

Researcher: You can say anything you want.

Voice: *(unintelligible\*) ...until we meet.*

*\*Words sound similar to, "I'll wait..."*

...................................................................................................

Recording made February 26, 2003
Lansing, Michigan

# Doing Something

·····································································

Researcher: Is there something you can do to make yourself known to me?

Voice: *I'm busy*

Researcher: I appreciate that you are trying to respond.

Voice: *I'm not.*

Researcher: Can I do anything to help you?

Voice: *I really need to finish this.*

·····································································

Recording made September 14, 2003
Grand Rapids, Michigan

# Elvis?

........................................................................

Researcher: I am happy to be here with you.

Voice: *Thank you.*

Researcher: I will stay here as long as I can.

Voice: *Thank you, very much.*

Researcher: Can you touch my shoulder?

Voice: *I know Karate.*

Researcher: Can you see this light?
(Turning on a flashlight)

Voice: *Trifari**

*Trifari is the brand name of a type of costume jewelry.*

........................................................................

Recording made August 11, 2000
Parma, Ohio

# Suess?

Researcher: You have nothing to
fear from me.

Voice: *I agree.*

Researcher: I only want to speak with you.

Voice: *So do.*

Researcher: Can you tap the table?

Voice: *I'm able.*

Researcher: I'll tap then you try. (tapping)

Voice: *Good bye.*

Researcher: Now you go.

Voice: *No.*

Recording made October 14, 1996
Sterling Heights, Michigan

# The Philosopher

........................................................................

Researcher: I am trying my best to contact you.

Voice: **We are closer than you know.**

Researcher: There is no reason to fear me.

Voice: **Fear is illusion.**

Researcher: Are you here with me?

Voice: **Everyone is here.**

*Responses translated from French.*

........................................................................

Recording made May 9, 2006
Windsor, Ontario, Canada

# The Teacher

........................................................................

Researcher: Is there anything you want
      us to do?

Voice: *Ask more questions.*

Researcher: Is there anything you want
      us to say?

Voice: *Speak to each other.*

Researcher: Can we do anything to help you?

Voice: *Learn more...*
(Small pause)
    *Read more, share thoughts.*

*Responses translated from German.*

........................................................................

Recording made March 26, 2001
Holland, Michigan

# Another Brat

........................................................................................

Researcher: If you can hear me can you knock like this...
*(Knocks on the floor twice)*

Voice: *(knocks three times)*

Researcher: Was that you can you knock twice?
*(Knocks on the floor twice)*

Voice: *(knocks three times)*

Researcher: I can't tell if that is you or something else so I'll move on.

Voice: ***It was something else.***

*(knocks three times)*

........................................................................................

Recording made January 9, 2004
Standish, Michigan

# Time Warp

..................................................................

Researcher: Is anyone here with me tonight?

Voice: *Now and later.*

Researcher: I'd like to attempt some sort of
communication with you.

Voice: *We did and will.*

Researcher: I don't mean to disturb you
and I don't intend to cause you
any harm.

Voice: *I knew that before you came.*

Researcher: Feel free to say anything at all.

Voice: *I did and shall.*

..................................................................

Recording made September 14, 1998
New York, New York

# Clumsy

........................................................................................

Researcher: Was that you who just knocked on the door?

Voice: ***Banged my elbow...***
(Small pause)
    ***Not Funny.***

Researcher: Could you knock on the door again?

Voice: ***Probably trip getting there.***

........................................................................................

Recording made April 23, 2005
Vega, Texas

# One Behind

Researcher: I am going to try and communicate with you. Is there any way you can communicate with me?

Voice: *(no response)*

Researcher: Can you tell me your name?

Voice: *I'll try.*

Researcher: Can you hear my words?

Voice: *Paul.*

Researcher: Am I bothering you?

Voice: *I can hear you.*

Researcher: You can say anything you like.

Voice: *No bother.*

*The name of the former owner of the location was Paul.*

Recording made July 10, 1996
Location withheld by client request.

# Ghost Dog?

Researcher: Are you the one who is moving objects around the house?

Voice: **The dog.**

Researcher: Is there someone with you or are you here alone?

Voice: **With the dog.**

Researcher: The family who now own this house do not want to be scared to live here anymore.

Voice: **The dog is scared.**

*The current owners of the home did not own a dog.*

Recording made November 13, 1995
Adrian, Michigan

# Not Evil

Researcher: Have you ever scratched a member of this family?

Voice: *Yes.*

Researcher: If you have then why are you hurting people?

Voice: *Getting attention.*

Researcher: The family thinks that you are mean or malicious.

Voice: *Not evil, lonely.*

Researcher: If you are scratching people can you please stop?

Voice: *Recognize me and yes.*

Recording made May 20, 1993
Clawson, Michigan

# Going Out

........................................................................

Researcher: Is there anyone here with us tonight?

Voice: *For a bit.*

Researcher: If so can you try and speak with us?

Voice: *Going out soon.*

Researcher: We would appreciate if you would try and contact us.

Voice: *Not now, plans.*

........................................................................

Recording made June 6, 2008
Auburn Hills, Michigan

The cassette tapes, pictured above were some of the recordings used in the process of compiling this book. Just these cassettes represent over 150 hours of E.V.P. recording sessions.

For quite a number of years this old Panasonic reel-to-reel recorder was the workhorse behind many E.V.P. sessions. It's never been retired and sometimes still shows up at investigations.

I usually try and perform an E.V.P. session in a room that has little to no furnishings. My basic protocol also demands multiple recording devices and as little movement from the experimenter as possible, which explains the giant pillow.

When performing E.V.P. session with large groups during events I usually discount most of the responses that are captured due to the amount of auditory pollution which can occur.
Photo by Tri-City Ghost Hunters Society - June 18, 2011: Historic Fort Wayne, Detroit, Michigan

# The Professor

......................................................................................

Researcher: I am attempting contact with anyone who may be here tonight.

Voice: *Please be more specific.*

Researcher: If you want to say anything, please feel free to do so.

Voice: *Math, physics or history?*

Researcher: We have instruments that will allow us to hear you.

Voice: *I am familiar with such technology.*

......................................................................................

Recording made May 17, 1994
Southfield, Michigan

# Inappropriate

......................................................................

Researcher: Feel free to tap my shoulder.

Voice: *Lower.*

Researcher: Is there anyone here with me?

Voice: *Touching your butt.*

......................................................................

Recording made December 5, 1999
Akron, Ohio

# Cartoons

..............................................................................................

Researcher: I was told you liked cartoons.

Voice: *Be very quiet.*

Researcher: Can you tell me about the cartoons you like?

Voice: *That's all folks.*

..............................................................................................

Recording made April 23, 2004
Steubenville, Ohio

# Many

. . . . . . . . . . . . . . . . . . . . . . . . . . . . . . . . . . . . . . . . . . . . . . . . . . . . .

Researcher: If you can hear me please feel free to speak to me. I won't be able to hear you now but I have a device which will allow me to hear you tomorrow. Is anyone here?

Voice 1: **Yes.**

Voice 2: **Present.**

Voice 3: **I am here.**

Voice 4: **Many are here.**

Researcher: Can you tell me your name?

Voice 3: **Too many here, confusing.**

Voice 1: **Too many speaking.**

*Each of the voices was distinctive enough to classify them as belonging to different entities.*

. . . . . . . . . . . . . . . . . . . . . . . . . . . . . . . . . . . . . . . . . . . . . . . . . . . . .

Recording made June 2, 2007
Lansing, Michigan

# Confusion

......................................................................

Researcher: Can you tell me your name?

Voice: *I forgot.*

Researcher: Can you tell me where you are?

Voice: *Can't remember.*

Researcher: You can say anything you want
to say I will not judge you.

Voice: *Jumbled thoughts, everything is
happening.*

......................................................................

Recording made May 19, 2001
Erie, Pennsylvania

# Joy

..........................................................................

Researcher: What are you feeling?

Voice: *So very happy ...joy.*

Researcher: What can you see?

Voice: (small laugh) *People crying.*

..........................................................................

Recording made August 3, 2007
Tuscon, Arizona

# Funhouse

..............................................................................

Researcher: Can you tell me what you
are seeing?

Voice: **Walls are moving.**

Researcher: Can you describe your
surroundings?

Voice: **No floor here...**
**Moving...**
**Everything is moving.**

..............................................................................

Recording made January 22, 2003
Kalamazoo, Michigan

# New Ghost?

.............................................................................

Researcher: Everyone present tonight would
like to speak to you.

Voice: **Hard to hear.**

Researcher: Feel free to say anything you
think needs to be said.

Voice: **It's like I'm floating.**

Researcher: We cannot hear you now, but we
will be able to hear you later.

Voice: **I could\* get used to this.**

*\* This word might be "would" or "should" the voice on the recording
cuts out during the first syllable.*

.............................................................................

Recording made May 6, 2000
Chicago, Illinois

# Addicted

........................................................................

Researcher: If there is anything I can do for you can you please let me know what it is?

Voice: **Cigarettes.**

Researcher: Will you help me to communicate with you?

Voice: **Bring Luckies\* next time.**

*\* This seems to be a reference to Lucky Strike cigarettes.*

........................................................................

Recording made August 16, 1997
Roseville, Michigan

# Aliens

·············································································

Researcher: I am here by myself is anyone with you?

Voice: *So many here.*

Researcher: Is there anyone you can recognize that is with you?

Voice: *So many familiar faces so many not human.*

Researcher: If someone is with you can you say their name?

Voice: *Outer space people even.*

·

·············································································

Recording made July 1, 1998
Grand Rapids, Michigan

# Brother?

..............................................................................................

Researcher: Do you want anything?

Voice: *Light.*

Researcher: Who are you?

Voice: *Widow's son.*

.

* *These responses seems to be Freemasonic in nature.*

..............................................................................................

Recording made May 4, 2000
Ferndale, Michigan

# Politician

..........................................................................................................

Researcher: Is there anything we can do
         for you?

Voice: **Vote.**

Researcher: Can you help us communicate
         with you?

Voice: **In November.**

Researcher: Why are you here?

Voice: **Promises.**

..........................................................................................................

Recording made July 14, 1997
Rose City, Michigan

# Funny but True

......................................................................

Researcher: This machine* can help us
 communicate.

Voice: *Like a telephone.*

Researcher: But I won't be able to hear you
 until tomorrow.

Voice: *Broken telephone.*

*\* The cassette recorder.*

......................................................................

Recording made July 3, 2002
Bay City, Michigan

# Ancient

· · · · · · · · · · · · · · · · · · · · · · · · · · · · · · · · · · · · · · · · · · · · · · · · · · · ·

Researcher: When did you die?

Voice: ***Your long ago.***

Researcher: Do you know what year it is?

Voice: ***(unintelligible response)***

Researcher: Did you live in this house?

Voice: ***Land before house.***

· · · · · · · · · · · · · · · · · · · · · · · · · · · · · · · · · · · · · · · · · · · · · · · · · · · ·

Recording made September 26, 1993
Garden City, Michigan

# Flux

························································

Researcher: What do you see?

Voice: *It's different... (pause)*
    *all changed.*

Researcher: Do you know where you are?

Voice: *Now, but then.*

························································

Recording made August 15, 1998
Tucumcari, New Mexico

# Forgiveness

........................................................

Researcher: Do you know who it was that
ended your life?

Voice: **Unimportant.**

Researcher: People are still interested in the
circumstances around your death.

Voice: **I'm not.**

Researcher: Is there anything we can do
for you?

Voice: **Forgive.**

........................................................

Date and location witheld by request of clients.

# Convert?

........................................................................

Researcher: What can I do for you?

Voice: ***Accept the Christ.***

Researcher: Do you know who you are?

Voice: ***Kneeling Indian.****

*\*The indigenous peoples of the Americas referred to themselves as "praying Indians" once they had been converted to Christianity. This might be another translation of that term.*

........................................................................

Recording made December 13, 2002
St. Ignace, Michigan

# That's called cheating.

........................................................................

Researcher: Can you see anything?

Voice: *The school\* ...students.*

Researcher: We are hoping you can help us communicate with you.

Voice: *Helping with exams.*

Researcher: Can you help us?

Voice: *Whispering.*

*\*Assumed to mean the campus of Michigan State University where the session was taking place.*

........................................................................

Recording made May 17, 2003
East Lansing, Michigan

# Joined

·············································································

Researcher: Is there anyone there
    around you?

Voice: ***Everywhere, always.***

Researcher: Are you there with anyone
    you know?

Voice: ***All together.***

Researcher: Can you see us here?

Voice: ***Here, there... will be.***

·············································································

Recording made April 27, 2001
Phoenix, Arizona

# Psychic

..................................................................

Researcher: Before I leave would you like to say anything?

Voice: *Flat highway.*

Researcher: I thank you for your time.

Voice: *You didn't hear me.*

*On the way home from this session my car struck a deep pothole. The next morning the front passenger's side tire was flat.*

..................................................................

Recording made January 10, 2004
Williamston, Michigan

# Musician

..........................................................................

Researcher: I would like to know more about who you are, or were.

Voice: *You play guitar.*

Researcher: If there is anything you want me to know feel free to say anything.

Voice: *I play the drums...(pause) played.*

*Responses translated from German.*

..........................................................................

Recording made December 24, 1997
Adrian, Michigan

# Conversation

..........................................................................

Researcher: I've been here for so long today I'm
going crazy...

Voice: **You can leave.**

Researcher: ...and now I'm sitting here talking about
myself out loud to myself.

Voice: **And me.**

Researcher: I wish a picture would fall off the wall or a
giant television materialized in front of me...

Voice: **Maybe you are crazy.**

Researcher: ...something, anything happen!

Voice: **It is.**

Researcher: Okay, let's start again. Can you tell me
your name?

Voice: **No longer matters... (pause)
not that name...(pause)
anymore.**

..........................................................................

Recording made November 9, 2005
Lake Orion, Michigan

# Full breakdown

..................................................................................................

For those people with an interest in some of the specifics of how most of these recording sessions happened I've decided to include this small transcript and further information. What you are about to read is a brief recap of the notes that were made in documenting the audio that was captured on July 26th, 2006 in Detroit, Michigan and can be found on page 15 of this book under the title of "Creepy."

| | |
|---|---|
| Equipment: | EV Electro Voice 9L95 Microphone |
| | Alesis 8-channel analog mixer with USB |
| | Audiovox Analog Cassette Recorder |
| Current Date/Time: | 07/26/2006 - 1:30 p.m. - 7:00 p.m. |
| Previous Date(s)/Time: | 07/22/2006 - 3:00 a.m. - 7:30 a.m. |
| | 06/28/2006 - 5:00 p.m. - 11:45 p.m. |
| | 06/25/2006 - 12:45 a.m. - 6:45 a.m. |
| | 06/20-21/2006 - 1:30 p.m. - 12:30 a.m. |

Fifth Audio Session:
-Begin tape-

1:30 p.m.
    I would like to speak with anyone who may be here with me.
1:33 p.m.
    (Truck outside, engine idling)
1:35 p.m.
    (Car horn)
1:37 p.m.
    My name is John and I would appreciate if you would try
    and speak to me.
1:40
    (Car passing outside)
1:42 p.m.
    I do not mean to cause any harm or any distress I would just like to
    talk to you.
1:46 p.m.
    (Car passing)
1:48 p.m.
    (Neighbor across the street door slam)
1:52 p.m.
    Can you tell me your name?

1:54 p.m.
    (Car passing)
1:56 p.m.
    (Water heater turned on)
2:00 p.m.
    Can you tell me how old you are?
2:05 p.m.
    (Change cassette)
2:12 p.m.
    Can you tell me what year it is?
2:15 p.m.
    (Water heater turned off)
2:20 p.m.
    I will be here with you until later tonight. Is that OK with you?
2:24 p.m.
    (Car passing)
2:28 p.m.
    (Car passing)

At this point you can see that over the period of an hour I've only made seven statements. Throughout the years I've found it sometimes takes a while to receive what may be a response and in order to not confuse a possible answer with a previous question time should be taken by the experimenter to allow conversation to happen. The responses in this case, as read on page 17, happened almost 5 hours after the session began.

6:15 p.m.
    Where do you think you are?
6:21 p.m.
    Response: In the forever.
6:24 p.m.
    Is anyone there with you?
6:26 p.m.
    (Car passing)
6:28 p.m.
    Response: All everyone no one.
6:31 p.m.
    What do you see where you are?
6:35 p.m.
    Response: The always.
6:37 p.m.
    (Dog outside barking)

# One last thing.

∙∙∙∙∙∙∙∙∙∙∙∙∙∙∙∙∙∙∙∙∙∙∙∙∙∙∙∙∙∙∙∙∙∙∙∙∙∙∙∙∙∙∙∙∙∙∙∙∙∙∙∙∙∙∙∙∙∙∙∙∙∙∙∙∙∙∙∙∙∙∙∙∙∙∙∙∙∙∙∙∙∙∙∙∙∙∙∙∙∙∙

Looking back over these pages it seems very odd to me that although this book is less than 60 total pages and contains no more than 10,000 words it took more than 20 years to write. I know that the internet is filled with well-intentioned persons who, almost daily, post what they believe are perfect "Class A" spirit voices[1] and while I admire their zeal and interest in phantalogical phenomena I do wish some of them would act in a more discerning manner. Many of the examples found in this book were taken from recordings made during investigations in which the original client had signed confidentiality agreements. Not only did I recontact those clients for permission to use examples from their cases but in numerous instances I chose to not include some of the more startling recordings due to the personal nature of the investigations. I also want to make it clear that some of these original recordings are available through me, for no charge, so that other researchers, and the generally interested, may examine them.

The formation of this book has one major goal; to instigate conversation, about not only the process of technological experiments with the so-called spirit world but about anomalistic phenomena in general. Hopefully you will find that even though the "conversations" printed in this work are short upon reflection they point toward deeper mysteries about the nature of our brief time in this reality. The words that are recorded and printed here were picked specifically to show the varying degrees of intellectual, emotional and spiritually differing aspects of the speakers. In some cases there were hours between answers, others carried on like a normal human conversation. Yet, as you read the words set down in these pages no matter how humanlike they sound we must remember that they may not have been spoken by humans. Researchers tend to forget that although "ghosts", and "spirits" may have been human beings at one time they are not, as far as we understand, human anymore. When we fully acknowledge the idea we may possibly be in communication with beings who are not any longer, or perhaps, never were human we can begin to evolve our day-to-day comprehension of how large, mysterious and beautiful this universe seems to be.

And for all the skeptics, all the 100% non-believers, all of the people who without question know for a fact that none of what is printed in this book could ever be true, I at least hope you found it funny.

I don't like to leave anyone out.

John E.L. Tenney

---

1 Class A examples of E.V.P. are those which are understandable and clearly heard by a person upon listening without audio manipulation.

# Further Reading

Bander, Peter,
Voices from the Tapes. New York: Drake Publishers Inc. 1973

Eisenbud, Jule,
The World of Ted Serios. New York: Wm. Morrow & Co., 1967

Fuller, John G.,
The Ghost of 29 Megacycles, New York: The New American Library Inc., 1981

Lodge, Oliver,
The Survival of Man, New York: George H. Doran Co., 1909

Pinker, Steven,
How the Mind Works, New York: W.W. Norton, 1999

Ramachandran, V.S.,
A Brief Tour of Human Consciousness, New York: Pi Press, 2004

Raudive, Konstantin,
Breakthrough. New York: Taplinger Publishing Co., 1971

Sherman, Harold,
The Dead are Alive. New York: Ballantine Books, 1981

Smith, Susy,
Voices of the Dead? New York: The New American Library Inc., 1977

## ABOUT THE AUTHOR

John E.L. Tenney has existed in many different forms on various planes of the multi-verse. In this reality he has chosen the persona of a human male born in Michigan during the 1970's. Although he has spent many years researching and investigating paranormal/supernatural phenomena he has also done stand-up comedy... like 3 times.

For more information or to contact the author please write to:
Weird Lectures
Post Office Box 1588
Royal Oak, MI 48068

# THANKS TO:

Mary Kathryn Fulton, Larissa Mrykalo, Brian Svendsen,
Laurie Reed, Elga Trejo, Rosalyn Michelle Bown, Amber Keller,
Genia Wamsley, B. Annette Durbin, Demented Warlok,
Maile TeresaBruns, Samuel Thomas Trivette, Nina De Santo,
Becky McClellan, Molli MClure, Essex County Ghost Project,
Atticus Evan Proulx, Donnie Irvin, Jennifer Fine Masterson,
Nicole Guy, Soraya Emanuels, Gareth Bartle, Michael "Mikey" McClain,
Kaiti Caillier, Kathy Kirk Alzubi, Christy Carrigan, Heaven Leigh Shelton,
Ashley Ackerman, Tracy Renee Carter, Lori Ann (Hillman) Moore,
Jeanette P. Hawe Applegate, Kristy Bodin, Melinda Kiper,
Michael Sinohui, Jacquelynne Smith, Gary Dill, Stephanie Sinohui,
Glen Eric Rutherford, Sara Vogel, Suzanne Ahmed,
Hannah Swartz, Mollie Christine Perez, Julie Pickel,
Tom Smith, Jacki Smith, Danielle Impagliazzo, Lisa Marie Cheek,
Cheryl Svendsen, Claudia Albitre, Pamela Hobbs,
Elizabeth Grieve, Janice Memory, Erin Paige,
Corey Hall, Eloise Roberts, Cory Stolberg, Jackie L. Mousseau,
Laura Love, TaraMarie Gignac, Laurie Reed, Amber Jenkins,
Kyle Cossell, John Bergman, Jr., Michael Franz,
Sandi Freeman, Heather Truan, Jason W.Stepp,
Cassie Lynch, Stephen MacPherson, Christian Logan,
Sarah E. Chrosniak, Louise Thompson, Matt Daniel,
Kenneth M. Logan, Adam G. Poole,
Ryan Nicole Shinzato, Rachel Fields

## SPECIAL THANKS:
Laura Eckert • Charlie
Johnny Houser • Greg Newkirk

Made in the USA
Lexington, KY
14 April 2013